Many thanks for your support:
Garbef Foundation

Supernose in London
© Baeschlin, Glarus 2025
A publishing house of the Lesestoff Group
Design: AS Grafik, Urs Bolz
Project management: Baeschlin Verlag, Gaby Ferndriger
Printing and binding: Druckhaus Sportflieger
ISBN: 978-3-03893-106-5
All rights reserved.

Visit us on the Internet:
www.baeschlinverlag.ch

Baeschlin is supported by the Federal Office of Culture for the years 2021–2024.

Author: Swantje Kammerecker has a degree in human medicine and has completed courses in CAS Communication for Nonprofit Organisations and at the College of Writing at the Axel Andersson Academy. She has been living in Switzerland for 25 years and works as an author, freelance copywriter, journalist and writing coach. She has already published ten books with Baeschlin Verlag, including seven children's books such as 'Vrenelisgärtli und andere Glarner Sagen', 'Der König des Waldes', 'Liam, Lara und die Furka-Dampfloks and 'Dr Kiddys Kidney Book' (English, German and French).

Illustrator: Ekaterina Chernetskaya was born in Moscow in 1978. After graduating from the Moscow State Architectural Institute MARchI, she worked as an architect and taught drawing at the same university. Since 2014, she has been associated with Switzerland, in particular the canton of Glarus. Her paintings can be found in private art collections in Switzerland as well as in Rome, Paris, London and New York. For Baeschlin Kinderbuchverlag, she has illustrated 'Die Bienenkönigin', 'Vom kleinen Hund, der lieber groß sein wollte', 'Leyla an der Glarner Landsgemeinde' as well as 'Luna, wie entsteht ein Buch', 'Dr Kiddy's Nierenbuch' and 'Nala und der Findelwolf'.

Orange
Bacon
Men's perfume
Peppermint chocolate
Blueberries
Popcorn
Leather
Women's perfume
Tea
Flower
Coffee
Bubble gum
Valerian
Question 1: Ratzia will hide in the handbag
Question 2: Suno smells the same men's perfume that was on the handkerchief

Swantje Kammerecker
Ekaterina Chernetskaya

SUPERNOSE IN LONDON

And this is how it works:
Thirteen fragrances are hidden in this book. So that you can smell them,
swipe your fingertip over the picture pages where there is no text,
preferably using a different fingertip. Then smell your fingertip.
You can try it out right away with the orange on this page.
Can you smell the orange?
If you can guess the other twelve scents in the book, you can find out
for yourself who stole the most important cat in the world.
Have fun smelling!

A new day is dawning in the London antique shop '1000 Treasures'.
Rhino Reich, the owner, is preparing a delicious breakfast with bacon.
Hmmm! The smell also awakens his detective dog Supernose, also called Suno.
Only a moment ago, he had been dreaming of a spectacular criminal hunt,
just like when he first met his master. The little stray dog had been lurking
around a market and caught a thief who had stolen the cash register
from Rhino. So they became best friends and Suno moved in with Rhino.
What paradise! Good food, a warm bed, attention, and a shop full of
great smells! The best part is that Rhino has set up a detective office in
the back room. Suno pricks up his ears when Rhino reads something out
of the newspaper. He's hoping for a new crime case. But what does he hear?
"Because a minister from China is coming to London, the city is under
heavy guard. The police ask people to stay calm. – Hmm, Suno, we will
hardly have any customers today. I think I'd rather go to the police auction
for lost valuables. Surely you can look after the shop for a while?"
Suno yelps: how boring! He would much rather come with us to the police...

Suno is sad and angry. Only one customer comes into the shop but doesn't want to buy anything. He only offers some supposedly valuable gemstones. But Suno immediately realises: these are just normal stones...!
When the dog is about to go back to sleep out of boredom, he suddenly hears a loud noise. He quickly jumps up and looks out of the shop. There's been a robbery in the chemist's next door! The staff and customers were stunned by a stink bomb and several people have fainted. Suno sees another fleeing figure and follows him. But the man has already jumped into a van and driven away. The only thing the thief loses is a handkerchief that smells of men's perfume, which the dog detective grabs. Back in the chemist's, Suno learns from the re-awakened pharmacist what was stolen: a newly-arrived shipment of fresh valerian herb! Valerian! The pharmacist calls the police, but they are too busy. To go out because of a box of valerian – how ridiculous!!

There is a lot of activity at 10 Downing Street, the Prime Minister's residence. Everything is getting cleaned and the Master of Ceremonies encourages Chief Mouser Cherry to catch the rodents in the house.
The Prime Minister is busy considering a gift for the state visit: it should be something typically British. An English racehorse? Too big! Precious tea? They have it in China too! "Oh, now I know: peppermint chocolate! But it has to be dusted with gold!" He immediately places the order. When the fine chocolate arrives, he has to try it himself! Hmmm! Many suppliers come and go; just one brings the floral decoration. Large boxes are carried into the house. And one disappears unnoticed – with a special content. When the Prime Minister wants to call his cat to come for a dress rehearsal, he finds that there is no trace of Cherry. A disaster! The whole house and the garden are searched feverishly. No Chief Mouser – but a strange suitcase is found in the bushes in front of the service entrance!

The police team is sitting together at the police station. The new police chief Heavymetal wants to restore proper order. "There are food scraps everywhere, no wonder the vermin come", he complains. As if to prove it, the police rat Ratzia appears, who usually helps herself modestly to the crumbs under the table. But today she can't resist the smell of fresh blueberry muffins.
By the way, Ratzia belongs to young Sergeant Bitterbeer and has always served him well in his investigations. A proven fighting rat with a talent for making herself invisible. This perfect undercover agent has already arrested several criminals and handed them over to the police.
But Heavymetal doesn't want to know about it! The rat has to go. In his anger he wants to grab Ratzia himself – but of course, she can run away and hide. Where?
You won't find that out so quickly!
(Question 1: Where will Ratzia hide? Read on!)

The police team is sitting together at the police station. The new police chief Heavymetal wants to restore proper order. "There are food scraps everywhere, no wonder the vermin come", he complains. As if to prove it, the police rat Ratzia appears, who usually helps herself modestly to the crumbs under the table. But today she can't resist the smell of fresh blueberry muffins.
By the way, Ratzia belongs to young Sergeant Bitterbeer and has always served him well in his investigations. A proven fighting rat with a talent for making herself invisible. This perfect undercover agent has already arrested several criminals and handed them over to the police.
But Heavymetal doesn't want to know about it! The rat has to go. In his anger he wants to grab Ratzia himself –
but of course, she can run away and hide. Where?
You won't find that out so quickly!
(Question 1: Where will Ratzia hide? Read on!)

Suno is running through the city. Valerian! Who steals something like that? And why? Very mysterious! Suno decides to explore the market where he has spent much of his life. He shows his detective ID to the traders and asks for the man with the valerian. But nobody knows anything. Finally, the dog detective is quite frustrated. One of the market traders gives him a box of popcorn to console him.

The alarm sounds at the police station! The Prime Minister's cat has been kidnapped! Cherry should have been present at the reception during the state visit, all smartened up. The ransom demand has already been received: £100,000! They wrote that if the amount hasn't arrived by 4:05 tomorrow morning, Cherry would never be seen again!
For delivering the money, the kidnappers have left a large old leather suitcase at the service entrance. The suitcase containing the ransom is to be left behind a certain tree in the dark park at Speakers Corner at 4:04 a.m. the following night. "And no police!" – Nevertheless, the police managed to have the suitcase picked up in a secret operation by a plainclothes policeman from Downing Street. It is now to be examined at the police station for possible traces that could lead to the culprit.

But in all the chaos at the police station, the suitcase unexpectedly ends up in the hall with the items to be auctioned. Rhino Reich is sitting there right now, yawning out of boredom. So far he hasn't bought anything at the auction – there was no hidden treasure among all the junk.
His annoyance increases even more when he sees the shadow of a dog he knows all too well appearing through the crack in the door. That's Suno! What's he doing here? He had specifically ordered him to stay in the shop.
At that moment the mysterious suitcase is offered for auction.
Nobody wants to bid for the ugly thing, not even Rhino. But then he sees Suno jumping onto the stage making loud howling sounds and wagging his tail.
His nose had raised the alarm: although to most people this suitcase only smells of leather – he's identified another scent!
(Question 2: Which scent? Read on!)
Rhino knows that his dog has a lead now. He buys the suitcase at the auction. And to make the whole action more discreet, he also buys the next item: a handbag smelling strongly of women's perfume,
suitable for the second-hand shop, thinks Rhino...

Outside again, Rhino and Suno watch as the streets near Buckingham Palace are decorated – with British and Chinese flags. Rhino is curious. Like many British people he loves pomp and celebrities and wants to have a look around. But Suno pulls his master towards home, then stops in front of the chemist's. Aha! Rhino knows that his dog realy has a lead now. He asks the pharmacist to explain what happened. Is the valerian theft related to the disappearance of Cherry the cat? And if so, how? At home, having tea with biscuits, Rhino turns on the TV to learn more about the mysterious cases: the kidnapping, the ransom demand, the suitcase…! With this exciting news, they don't even notice that the auctioned handbag has moved next to the suitcase! Whoops! When Rhino opens it, a rat crawls out!! But she is actually very nice and tame. The two of them offer her a biscuit.
While they are still sitting in front of the suitcase, a little confused, the rat whispers something in Suno's ear! The dog grabs the suitcase and together the two trot into the second-hand shop's storage area.
    Rhino is surprised: well, what kind of plan do they have?

It's late at night as Rhino and Suno sneak through London's streets. Rhino is carrying the suitcase. They are promptly stopped by the police, who arrest Rhino! Suno is just able to grab the suitcase and flee with it in the direction of the park for the planned handover of the ransom. At about four o'clock in the morning, he drops off the suitcase in the designated place and hides behind a tree. Then, he sees a figure approaching from the darkness with a barrow of flowers. The florist finds the suitcase, opens it briefly and seems satisfied, then quickly closes it again and puts it beneath the flowers on the barrow. He doesn't notice that Suno is following him. They zigzag through small alleys; apparently, the man wants to remain inconspicuous. Finally, they reach the market square. There some traders are already unloading goods and setting up their stalls. The suspect stops at a van with a flower picture.

At the police station, it smells strongly of coffee. This keeps young Sergeant Bitterbeer awake while he interrogates Rhino.
"Why did you want the suitcase? Were you involved in the kidnapping of the cat?" Rhino claims his innocence. "I bought the suitcase from you, from the police! But it smelled so bad that I was going to dump it." – "Haven't you heard or read the news? The suitcase is our only lead to the kidnapper!" – Rhino shakes his head: "The only lead? No. There's one more thing: valerian." – "What do you mean, valerian?" – "I'm pretty sure Cherry was kidnapped with the help of valerian. The herb completely turns cats' heads. If they smell it, they follow you blindly. Someone must have lured him with it; otherwise, he would never have left his home!" – "Aha!" Bitterbeer suddenly sounds interested: "So that means valerian could help to find the cat again?" – "Why not?" – "Okay, Mr Rhino. If you help us, you can now have some coffee – and if you succeed, then you'll be free!"

Cherry is sitting in a small cage in the florist's van. He's angry that he fell for that stupid valerian! His guard in the front of the vehicle has just dozed off when his accomplice opens the driver's door: "Hey, man, we've got the money! Let's bring back the fat cat now while it's still dark." – "Yes, brother, but first let's check that everything is clean." In the twilight, they open the suitcase and see a lot of pound notes. As the kidnapper jubilantly reaches into the suitcase with both hands, there is a cry of pain: Ratzia has been hiding under the fake money and now bites his finger hard. At the same time, Suno goes on the attack and grabs the accomplice's leg. There is commotion in the vehicle. The cage with the cat flips over and rolls across the marketplace, heading for the Thames... The fighters stumble, tear down stalls, causing huge chaos in the market. The traders complain and call the police. Suno and Ratzia hold the crooks with relentless force until the police arrive.
There! Finally! Bang! But don't worry, it wasn't a shot, just the popping of Sergeant Bitterbeer's bubble gum!

The Chinese minister has arrived and is on his way to his first meeting: breakfast with the Queen. Afterwards, there will be a lunch with the Prime Minister in Downing Street. Everything is ready – only Cherry is missing! Meanwhile, chaos is spreading on London's streets. The police had the glorious idea of laying valerian everywhere to attract Cherry, and lo and behold: hordes of cats came running and blocked everything. But there was no sign of the cat they were looking for! The police have to work hard to clear the streets. And Cherry? Suno and Ratzia were able to free him from the cage after handing over the two criminals to the police. They found the cat just in time; he almost fell into the Thames! Escorted by Suno and Ratzia, Cherry finally arrives back at Downing Street. There, the heroic animals are given a great welcome and even receive a medal. Rhino, who is now back at home and is missing his dog very much, is amazed when he sees him on TV during a live broadcast of the state reception. He's extremely proud of the dog detective who's waving his hat at him from the screen. "My faithful Suno!! Good boy! Come home, I'll fry some bacon for us!" he calls, knowing he won't have to wait long for his much-loved dog.